Christ Revealed in the New Testament

Witness Lee

Living Stream Ministry
Anaheim, California

First Edition, 6,500 copies. June 1989.

ISBN 0-87083-469-X

Published by

Living Stream Ministry
1853 W. Ball Road, Anaheim, CA 92804 U.S.A.
P. O. Box 2121, Anaheim, CA 92814 U.S.A.

Printed in the United States of America

CONTENTS

FOREWORD

The following messages were given by Brother Witness Lee in May of 1984 at a Chinese conference in New York City. The present book is translated from the Chinese. It covers specifically the subject of Christ as revealed in the New Testament.

Christ is the center of the whole Bible. In particular He is the subject of the New Testament. Our brother has released this timely truth in simple, concise words according to the pure revelation of the Bible and based upon his accumulated light of fifty years of study. They are now available for the enjoyment and appreciation by the saints. The outline of every message is printed at the beginning of every chapter. They are, in the author's words, the essence of the New Testament. May the Lord breathe His breath and anoint His Spirit upon these words.

CHAPTER ONE

CHRIST IN THE GOSPELS

Scripture Reading: Luke 1:35; Matt. 1:20; John 1:14; 14:9, 10; Matt. 3:16; Luke 4:1, 14; Matt. 27:45, 46; Luke 24:5, 6; John 20:22

OUTLINE

I. Christ was conceived of the Holy Spirit of God in the womb of a chaste virgin and born with both the nature of God and of man, being the complete God and perfect Man, a God-man in whom God and man are mingled—Luke 1:35; Matt. 1:20.

II. The Triune God, as the Son coming from and with the Father and by the Spirit, became a man of flesh on earth—John 1:14; 1 Tim. 3:16. This Triune God—the Father, the Son, and the Spirit—coexists and coinheres in this flesh—John 8:29; 14:9, 10. The Son is one with the Father, living by the Father, working with the Father, speaking the Father's word, and doing the Father's will—John 10:30; 6:57; 5:19; 14:24; 6:38.

III. The fullness of the Godhead of the Triune God dwells in Him bodily. He is the embodiment of the Triune God—Col. 2:9.

IV. As far as God's essence is concerned, the Spirit of God was in Him at the time of His conception to be His divine element for the existence of this God-man; but as far as God's economy is concerned, when He was thirty years of age, the Spirit of God descended upon Him to be His power for the work of the Christ, God's anointed—Matt. 3:16; Luke 4:18, 19.

V. He lived and moved according to the Spirit of God and also worked and fought by the Spirit of God—Luke 4:1, 14; Matt. 12:28.

VI. The Triune God—the Son as the good shepherd, the Spirit as the fine woman, and the Father as the loving father—works together to seek, save, and receive the repentant sinners who turn to Him—Luke 15:3-32.

VII. The Triune God, the Son with the Father and by the Spirit, died and shed His blood for the sinners in the flesh of Jesus' humanity, accomplishing the eternal redemption—Rom. 8:3; 2 Cor. 5:21; 1 Cor. 15:3; Heb. 9:14, 12.

VIII. When He died on the cross to accomplish redemption for sinners, God forsook Him according to God's economy (Matt. 27:45, 46), but God went through the death of the cross with Him according to God's essence. Hence, according to His humanity in the flesh He was put to death; but according to His divinity in the spirit He was made alive—1 Pet. 3:18.

IX. The blood of this God-man shed on the cross is the blood of Jesus the Son of God—1 John 1:7. The blood of Jesus is genuine human blood; it is qualified to redeem man from sin. His unlimited divinity made the redeeming efficacy of the blood of Jesus the Son of God both eternal and unlimited.

X. This God-man entered death, passed through death, overcame death, and resurrected from death with His body, making His body a resurrected spiritual body—John 10:18; Acts 2:23, 24; Luke 24:5, 6; 1 Cor. 15:44.

XI. This last Adam who died and resurrected passed through death and resurrection to become a life-giving Spirit (1 Cor. 15:45) and is breathed as air into those who believe in Him to be their life and essence—John 20:22. In this way, this Triune God—the Father, the Son, and the Spirit—who became flesh, passed through death, and entered into resurrection, is in them to be with them forever—John 14:16, 17, 20, 24; Matt. 28:20.

This time in New York I am very happy to see so many scattered countrymen and brothers and sisters who are residing on the east coast of America. It is a rare opportunity for us to meet together and to fellowship in life before the Lord. I truly have a burden and feeling within me to fellowship with all of you concerning the Christ revealed in the New Testament. In the six thousand years of human history, no one has been able to surpass this mysterious Christ. He is the unique and extraordinary One. The more I preach Him, the more I feel that He is so mysterious, yet sweet. Although I cannot explain Him thoroughly, the more I speak of Him the more I enjoy Him. For this reason by His grace I will speak about Him during this short period of time in a clear way and with simple words according to the revelation I have received and the light I have accumulated throughout the years. The more clearly and deeply we know Him, the stronger will be our love towards Him. May He grant us a sober mind and an open spirit that we would know Him through the revelation in the spirit.

The central revelation of the Bible, and particularly of the New Testament, is this mysterious Christ. We need four messages to cover the Christ as revealed in the New Testament: the Christ in the Gospels, the Christ in Acts, the Christ in the Epistles, and the Christ in Revelation. In order to strengthen your understanding of the messages, and in order to deepen your realization of the Lord, I have purposely prepared four printed outlines and have given them to you. These four outlines can be considered as the marrow and essence of the whole New Testament. I hope that you can make as many copies of these outlines as possible and send them to your friends and relatives in the Lord so that all of God's children may have a clearer, richer, and sharper understanding of this mysterious Christ through the revelation in the spirit. By this we will love Him in a deeper and more sincere way from within. The four Gospels speak specifically about Christ. The first outline covers this Christ in the Gospels. There are altogether eleven points. This is the essence of my fifty years of studying and expounding the four Gospels. This outline presents to you the wonderful Person described and revealed in the four Gospels, Jesus Christ the Son of God. I believe after we see these eleven points, we will have a clear picture of this wonderful Person revealed in the four Gospels.

CONCEIVED OF THE HOLY SPIRIT AND BORN OF A VIRGIN

The first item of the outline says that this wonderful Person, Jesus Christ, was conceived of the Holy Spirit of God in the womb of a chaste virgin. We all know that whenever we come to the biography of a man we have to mention his origin. The origin of Jesus Christ is, on the one hand, God, and on the other hand, man. His conception was by the Holy Spirit of God and in the womb of a chaste virgin. This is very difficult to understand and is very mysterious. According to the meaning of the Bible, the Holy Spirit of God is just God Himself. Therefore, for Him to be conceived by the Holy Spirit in the womb of a chaste virgin is to be conceived through the coming of God Himself into a chaste virgin. Naturally, with this conception there are both the elements of God and man. With the Holy Spirit there is the element of God, and with the virgin there is the element of man. As a result, this conception produced the One who is a God-man.

HAVING BOTH GOD AND MAN AS HIS ESSENCE

Item number one of the outline continues by saying that He was born with both the nature of God and of man. This is very difficult to understand, yet it is a fact. Jesus Christ possesses not only divinity, but also humanity. He possesses both divinity and humanity at the same time. The divinity and humanity refer not only to His nature, but also to His essence. The essence of Jesus Christ is divinity as well as humanity. He is a God-man, in whom divinity was added to humanity, that is, in whom the essence of God was added to the essence of man. Hence, He is the complete God as well as the perfect Man.

From God's side He is fully God and from man's side He is truly man. He is the God-man in whom both God and man are mingled as one. We all know that conception is a kind of mingling. How is a conception possible without the mingling? In the conception of Jesus Christ there were two essences: the essence of God and the essence of man. The two were not just added together; they were mingled together. The One produced from this mingling is a God-man.

BEING THE TRIUNE GOD

The second item of the outline says that the Creator of the universe, the unique God of the heavens and the earth, is the Triune God. In traditional Christian theology, He is called the Trinity. In recent years we have investigated and studied the matter and have found out that the word "trinity" comes from Latin. The theological expression "three persons in one essence" in English is derived from Latin. In Latin the word used is not "person" or "persons," but "persona" or "personae." Here we have a fine distinction in theology. Some authorities say that the word "persona" in Latin means the mask worn by the actors in a play. The same person would at one time put on the mask of an old man and after a few minutes put on the mask of a child; then a few minutes later he may put on the mask of an old woman. After much studying we cannot agree with this kind of teaching of the trinity. For this reason we dropped the word "trinity." Instead we use the word "triune." The word triune is a proper term in theology. Although we cannot find this term in the Bible, there is nonetheless the fact and the description. The term was invented by students of the Bible for the proper expression of the matter. Theologians throughout the ages have used this term. It is a Latin compound word "tri-une" anglicized. "Tri" means three and "une" means one. Hence triune means "three-one." What does it mean to be triune? It just means triune. One cannot explain it. This is exactly what it means. It cannot be explained. If it can be explained then it is no longer real and mysterious. Some have added the word "in" to read "three in one." But strictly speaking it is not three in one, but three-one. Then what is the meaning of three-one? I have studied much and have read a lot of writings by others with the hope that I could explain the matter more clearly. In the end I found out that no one can explain it clearly. Someone once asked Martin Luther, "What is three-one?" He answered: "I do not know. If I knew, I would be God." He was not God; therefore, he did not know. This is right. Do not think that we know everything. We are not even clear concerning the structure of our own human body. How then can we understand the Triune God? But the pure Word of God, which is the Bible, shows us that our God is the Triune God. He is the Father, the Son, and the Spirit. He is God the Father, God the Son, and God the Spirit.

Following this, item two of the outline says that this Triune God, as the Son coming from and with the Father (the word "from" in John 6:46 carries with it the meaning of "with") and by the Spirit, became a man of flesh on earth. This word is difficult to understand. The Triune God is the Father, the Son, and the Spirit. He is three, yet He is one God. This God became a man in the flesh. His coming was the Son's coming, but the Son's coming was from and with the Father. Hence, the Son's coming brought with Him the Father's coming. Moreover, this coming is by the Spirit. John 8:29 shows us clearly that the Father has not only sent the Son; He came with the Son as well. The Son was never alone on earth; the Father was with Him all the time. This Triune God—the Father, the Son, and the Spirit—coexists and coinheres in the flesh of the Lord Jesus. This One is in that One, and the Two are in the third One. The third One is in turn in the first and the second One. The Three coinhere one in another. In John 14:10 the Lord said, "I am in the Father, and the Father is in Me." This word "coinherence" is a special term used in theology. The night before last I was in Newton, Massachusetts. I gave a message in English using the word "coinherence." One professor in Biblical Greek, a man over sixty years of age, was among the audience. His textbook on Greek is the second most popular one in the United States. When he heard me using the term "coinherence," he was very surprised that an old Chinese would speak about theology in America using the word "coinherence." He said that most theologians in America do not use this term anymore because it is too deep and is too difficult to clarify. But this is a truth in the Bible! We should not be afraid of difficulty and should not let this word go by easily. Rather, we should study this word thoroughly. We all love the Lord, but we should not love Him in a blind way. We all have to seek after a deep understanding of the Lord. The more deeply we know Him, the more thoroughly we will love Him.

THE FATHER, THE SON, AND THE SPIRIT BEING ONE

Item number two continues by saying that the Son is one with the Father. He lives because of the Father. "Because" means "by." He does not live by Himself, rather He lives by the Father. He works with the Father, speaking the Father's word and doing the Father's will. The Son's words are the Father's words, and the Son's work is the Father's work. It seems as if the Son has nothing of His own. The Two do not have two speakings, but one speaking. The Two do not have two works, but one work. And the Two have only one will. The reason for this is because They are just one. Why then is there the distinction of two? Why is there the Father and the Son? This is very mysterious and is difficult to understand. All orthodox theologians agree that although the Father, the Son, and the Spirit are of three, yet They are one. But as to how one are the Three, no one can draw the line. We can only receive the revelation of the Bible according to its literal text. Matthew 28:19 clearly says the Father, the Son, and the Holy Spirit, but the Three have only one singular name. This shows us that the Father, the Son, and the Spirit are one. Although the Triune God has the distinction of the Father, the Son, and the Spirit, still They cannot be separated; there is still one God. The Lord Jesus that we believe in is not only the Son, but is also the Father. Isaiah 9:6

says that a son is given unto us and that His name is called the everlasting Father. The reason for this is that the Father and the Son are one (John 10:30). John 5:43 says that the Son came in the name of the Father. It was the Son coming; but He came in the name of the Father. Who then came? Was it the Father or the Son? The answer is that the Two are one. The Son's coming was the Father's coming. In our concept we always consider that the Son is in us, and that the Father is on the throne. But in reality both the Father and the Son are in us, and at the same time both are also on the throne. The Son and the Father can never be separated. The Son's being in us is the Father's being in us. The Father's being on the throne is the Son's being on the throne. They are not two separate persons, one here and the other there.

A DISTINCTION BETWEEN ESSENCE AND ECONOMY

Item number three says that the fullness of the Godhead of the Triune God dwells in Him bodily. He is the Father, the Son, and the Spirit, and He came to earth to be a man of flesh. Hence, He is the embodiment of the Triune God. The Godhead is not just the Son, nor is it just the Father, nor just the Spirit. Rather, it is the Godhead of the Triune God—the Father, the Son, and the Spirit.

Item four says that as far as God's essence is concerned, the Spirit of God was in Him at the time of His conception to be His divine element for the existence of this God-man; but as far as God's economy is concerned, when He was thirty years of age, the Spirit of God descended upon Him to be His power for the work of Christ, God's anointed. When the Lord Jesus was born, the Spirit was already in Him as His essence. But when He was thirty years old the Spirit came upon Him again. I never could understand this point. He was born of the Holy Spirit; the Spirit was already in Him. Why then did the Spirit come upon Him again at the age of thirty? Not until the recent years when I studied the Bible again did I understand that there is the distinction between the essential and the economical aspects. Essentially speaking, the Holy Spirit as the Spirit of life was in Him for His existence; economically speaking, the Holy Spirit as the Spirit of power came upon Him for His work.

Item five says that He lived and moved according to the Spirit of God and also worked and fought by the Spirit of God. This means that at the birth of the Lord Jesus, the Holy Spirit was in Him as His essence. At the age of thirty, when He came out to fulfill His ministry, the Holy Spirit came again, not as His essence within, but upon Him as power without, for the fulfillment of His ministry for the accomplishment of God's economy. He had the Holy Spirit within Him as His life, and He had the Holy Spirit without as His power. In this way, He was able to live and move according to the Spirit of God. His daily life was full of the Holy Spirit and was led by the Holy Spirit. At the same time He worked, fought, and defeated the Devil for God also by the Holy Spirit. Luke 4:18-19 says that He preached the gospel by the Holy Spirit. Matthew 12:28 says that He cast out demons by the Holy Spirit. As the omnipotent One, why did He have to work and fight by the Holy Spirit? This is because it is a matter of God's economy. As far as His essence is concerned, He and the Holy Spirit are one. This omnipotent One is the Holy Spirit, for the Father, the Son, and the Spirit are but one God.

THE FATHER, THE SON, AND THE SPIRIT WORKING TOGETHER TO ENABLE THE SINNER TO ENJOY GOD'S ETERNAL SALVATION

Item number six says that the Triune God—the Son as the good shepherd, the Spirit as the fine woman, and the Father as the loving father—work together to seek, save, and receive the repentant sinners who turn to Him. In Luke 15 we have first a good shepherd that came to seek for the lost sheep. Next we have a fine woman that sought for the lost coin. These two seekings brought the sinner back, resulting in a loving father receiving the prodigal son. The prodigal son came to his senses, not due to himself, but due to the woman, who is the Spirit, whose enlightening is based on the good shepherd's seeking. This results in the prodigal son coming to himself and returning. Finally, we even see the loving, waiting father receiving him back to his home. In this chapter we see the Triune God. The Son is the good shepherd, the Spirit is the fine woman, and the Father is the loving father. The Son came to redeem, the Spirit came to seek, then the repentant sinner returns to the Father. Once the sinner repents to the Father, he is brought back in the Son to the Father, and the Father receives him with His loving hand. In this way we are brought back to the Father's house to enjoy the eternal love of the Father. This is the Son, the Spirit, and the Father, the Three working and cooperating together to seek, save, and receive the repentant sinner.

Item number seven says that the Triune God, the Son with the Father and by the Spirit, died and shed His blood for the sinners in the flesh of Jesus' humanity, accomplishing the eternal redemption. Often we say that Jesus Christ died for us, yet we do not realize that the One who died for us is the Son with the Father by the Spirit. It was not just Jesus Christ who died for us; rather, it was the whole Triune God who died for us in the human flesh. This is a very mysterious matter, but it is all based on the Scriptures. You can read carefully Romans 8:3, 2 Corinthians 5:21, 1 Corinthians 15:3, and Hebrews 9:14, 12.

DYING IN FLESH, BEING MADE ALIVE IN SPIRIT

Item number eight says that when the Lord Jesus died on the cross to accomplish redemption for sinners, God forsook Him according to God's economy. This was why He cried, "My God, My God, why have You forsaken Me?" (Matt. 27:46). On the cross He bore our sins and even became sin for us, suffering the righteous judgment of God. At that moment, God forsook Him as far as God's economy is concerned. But as far as God's essence is concerned, God was passing through the death of the cross together with Him, for the essence of God was forever in Him; it never departed from Him. Hence, according to His humanity in the flesh He was indeed crucified on the cross. But according to the Spirit of holiness, He was made even more alive! This is why 1 Peter 3:18 says, "Being put to death in flesh, but made alive in spirit." Not only was His spirit made alive; verse 19 of the same chapter even says that by this spirit He went to prison to proclaim to the rebellious ones His victory. When the Lord Jesus died on the cross, it was the flesh of humanity that died shedding the human blood, but the divine Spirit was not put to death. On the contrary, it was made more alive.

THE BLOOD OF JESUS THE SON OF GOD BEING ETERNALLY EFFICACIOUS

Item number nine says that the blood of this God-man shed on the cross is the blood of Jesus the Son of God. First John 1:7 says, "The blood of Jesus His Son cleanses us from all sin." The blood of Jesus is genuine human blood. It was man that sinned; therefore, only the blood of man can cleanse the sins of man. Jesus was a man. The blood that He shed was genuine human blood and was qualified to redeem man from his sins. Not only so, here it does not say that this is "the blood of Jesus the Son of Man"; rather, it says that it is "the blood of Jesus the Son of God." This proves that the human blood shed by Jesus has the guarantee of the unlimited power of God's divinity. His unlimited divinity has made the redeeming efficacy of the human blood that He shed both eternal and unlimited. Therefore, the redemption that Christ has accomplished is an eternal redemption.

The death of the Lord Jesus is the death passed through by both God and man. The human blood that He shed is able to redeem man from sin. But this blood is also the blood of Jesus the Son of God which has the unlimited divinity of God, and it has made this redemption eternally efficacious. He died once for all, shedding His blood to redeem all those who believe in Him throughout the ages. The efficacy of the blood of Jesus the Son of God is universal, eternal, and it is not limited by time, space, or function.

HAVING DIED AND RESURRECTED TO BECOME
A RESURRECTED SPIRITUAL BODY

Item number ten says that this God-man entered death, passed through death, and overcame death. The death of the Lord Jesus on the cross was a voluntary one. He said, "No one takes it [My life] away from Me, but I lay it down of Myself. I have authority to lay it down, and I have authority to take it again" (John 10:18). Although the Lord Jesus died, He was resurrected. He walked into death boldly and without hesitation, and He also walked out of death boldly and without hesitation. He entered death, passed through death, overcame death, and resurrected from death in His flesh, that His flesh might become a resurrected spiritual body. This is not easy to explain. We need an illustration to clarify it. For example, if we bury a tiny, dark carnation seed into the ground, it dies in the ground. At the same time it also germinates in the ground. The death and germination of this seed is a good illustration of death and resurrection. The green sprout is a transformed form of the flower seed. Although the shape has changed, its essence remains the same. Later the sprout grows to blossom, and the shape is further transformed in resurrection. Yet its essence is still the same as the seed's. The Lord Jesus said, "Unless a grain of wheat falls into the ground and dies, it abides alone; but if it dies, it bears much fruit" (John 12:24). The Lord is the grain of wheat that entered into death. In resurrection He grew up to produce many grains. This is His death and resurrection.

THE PNEUMATIC CHRIST

Item eleven says that this last Adam who died and resurrected passed through death and resurrection to become a life-giving Spirit. This is based on the word in 1 Corinthians 15:45. This life-giving Spirit is breathed into the believers as air, to be their life and essence. John 20:22 shows us that after the Lord's resurrection He came in the midst of His disciples to breathe into them. His breathing is the exhaling of Himself which is also our inhaling. This breath is a holy breath, which is also the Holy Spirit, indicated by the Greek word *pneuma*. This word means breath. It also means spirit, or wind. The adjective in English is pneumatic, which means to be full of air. After the Lord Jesus died and resurrected, He became a pneuma. Hence, in theology there is such a term, the pneumatic Christ. This Christ is the Spirit; therefore, He can breathe Himself into the disciples to be their life and essence. This Lord who has passed through death and has entered into resurrection is the Triune God, the Father, the Son, and the Spirit, and is within the disciples to be with them forever. This is the Jesus described in the four Gospels.

From His conception, Christ passed through His birth, His living on earth, His death, and His resurrection to become the Spirit of life to enter into the believers as their life. Such a pneumatic Christ is the Christ revealed in the four Gospels. May this complete picture show you what a person the Lord Jesus is in the four Gospels. He is the Triune God entering into the womb of a chaste virgin to be conceived and born. He is God and also man. He has the essence of God, yet He lived on earth for thirty-three and a half years in humanity for God's economy. In Him there is the Holy Spirit as the essence, and upon Him there is the Holy Spirit as the power. He entered death, passed through death, and overcame death. Finally, He was resurrected from death to become the pneumatic Christ to enter into us who believe in Him, to be our life and essence. In this way we enjoy the Triune God, the Father, the Son, and the Spirit, in us to be with us all the time as our everything.

Chapter Two

CHRIST IN THE ACTS

Scripture Reading: Acts 1:3-5, 8-9, 12-14; 2:1-4, 16-18; 4:8, 31; 13:9, 52; 6:3, 5; 7:55; 11:24; 8:29, 39; 13:2; 16:6-7

OUTLINE

I. In His resurrection, after breathing Himself as breath into those who believed in Him, He was physically with them for forty days, sometimes appearing and sometimes disappearing to train them to be accustomed to His invisible presence so that they would realize the kingdom of God as the reality and sphere of the living of the divine life—John 20:26; 21:1; Acts 1:3.

II. After charging the disciples to wait for the Spirit promised by the Father to fall on them so that they could be His witnesses unto the uttermost parts of the earth, He visibly departed from them according to God's economy and was taken up into heaven—Acts 1:4-9.

III. As far as God's essence is concerned, He was still with the disciples by being in them. Hence, they were able to withstand the threat of the Jews and remain in Jerusalem to wait for the promised Spirit of power from God, and the one hundred and twenty people were able to pray in one accord for ten days, cooperating with God's administration in heaven to bring in the great act of God at Pentecost—Acts 1:12-14.

IV. At Pentecost this exalted God-man, who has ascended to the throne to be made Lord and Christ and Head of all things by God (Acts 2:33, 36; Eph. 1:22), poured Himself out as the Spirit of power on those disciples who had already received Him as the

Spirit of life and who were waiting for the Spirit of power. In this way the ascended Head baptized His Body into Himself as the all-inclusive Spirit— Acts 2:1-4, 16-18.

V. From now on those who believe in Him are filled outwardly with His Spirit of power (Acts 2:4; 4:8, 31; 13:9), and they are filled inwardly with His Spirit of life (Acts 13:52) to be inwardly full of His Spirit (Acts 6:3, 5; 7:55; 11:24), becoming a group of people mingled as one with this all-inclusive Spirit. He is in them as the Spirit of life to be lived out of them to express Himself. He is also outside of them as the Spirit of power to be preached and propagated by them as His continuation and spread on the earth.

VI. Those who are filled and saturated with His all-inclusive Spirit within and who are filled and equipped without are led by Him to spread His kingdom on earth that His church may be established—Acts 8:29, 39; 13:2; 16:6, 7.

KNOWING THE TRIUNE GOD THROUGH REVELATION

The Triune God cannot be analyzed by our limited logic and wisdom. The Bible gives us the fact of the Triune God, but if man tries to understand Him by analysis and deduction, he will be like a blind man touching an elephant; what he touches will be only a little part of the whole elephant, and he will still be very unclear. The Bible is not for man to reason with. It is a book of revelation. Only by revelation will man know the mysterious part of the Bible, that is, the Triune God. First, revelation includes facts. For example, tonight I am standing here and all of you are sitting there; this is a fact. Second, there is the light. With the fact, there is the light. In addition, there is the third matter, a healthy sight. When you put the three together, you have revelation. Although the Bible is not for us to reason with, but is rather for us to see, we need to see it without any colored glasses. Many times, although man has all three of the above matters, he looks into the pure, clean word of God with a pair of black glasses. As a result, the Bible appears black. The Bible is not black. It is the glasses that are black. What man needs is to change his glasses. We must have revelation. It is through revelation that we can understand with a pure mind and an open spirit the deep truth concerning the Triune God.

The Lord's recovery began sixty-two years ago in 1922 in Foochow, the hometown of Brother Watchman Nee. From mainland China we spread to Taiwan and then to America. We have always given people a strong impression that among us we emphasize the truth very much. The Lord's recovery among us can be considered a recovery of truths. From the first day until now, not only have we not changed our attitude, rather, we have strengthened it. I hope very much that through these four messages and by revelation, we can have a deeper understanding of the Triune God. We should not be shallow Christians, saying what others say in a superficial way. Rather, we should be equipped by the truth of Christ that we may become those who preach this truth.

DIFFERENT TEACHINGS
CONCERNING THE DIVINE TRINITY

So far, there have been three categories of teachings concerning the divine Trinity. The first is modalism, the second is tritheism, and the third is the revelation concerning the divine Trinity. Both the first and the second are heretical teachings. Only the third is correct according to the proper revelation of the Bible.

When the theologians debated about the persons of the Trinity during the second and third centuries, one group asserted that the Father, Son, and Spirit are just one God and that They have appeared in three different modes at different times and places. So this school of teaching is called modalism, and those that held to this teaching were called the modalists. The strongest proponent of this teaching was Sabellius. Hence, in proper church history, his teaching, Sabellianism, is also known as modalism. He asserted that God is three and one. This is correct. But he said that in the Old Testament, God was the Father; in the New Testament in the Gospels, the Son came, and the Father ceased to exist. In other words, in the Gospels the Father became the Son. During this period only the Son existed; the Father did not exist anymore. In the Acts, the Epistles, and Revelation, the Spirit came, and the Son ceased to exist. The Son became the Spirit. During this period only the Spirit existed. Both the Father and the Son had ceased to exist. For this reason there are three modes of God: the mode of the Father, the mode of the Son, and the mode of the Spirit. These three modes are not simultaneous but appear consecutively one after another. When the second came, the first passed away. And when the third came, the second was over. This is a great heresy.

From the second and third centuries on, another group of people rose up to oppose modalism. They strongly asserted that the Father, the Son, and the Spirit are three different persons, that they are distinct as well as separate yet existing simultaneously at any one time. This kind of teaching resulted in tritheism, and it formed an extreme contrast to modalism. Modalism stood in one extreme, while tritheism stood in another. Both are heresies. Orthodox theology rejects both of these kinds of teachings. In A. D. 325 the Council of Nicaea and its subsequent creed avoided these two kinds of extremes.

I have clearly presented before you the essence of the four Gospels. You can see that we do not believe in modalism or in tritheism but in the revelation of the divine Trinity. In the Old Testament, the Father, the Son, and the Spirit were all there. Genesis 1:1 says that in the beginning God created the heavens and the earth. God was there. Then verse 2 says that the Spirit of God brooded over the water. The Spirit of God was also there. By chapter eighteen, there were three men who appeared to Abraham. One of them was the Lord Jesus. He appeared as a man, and Abraham washed His feet and served Him a feast. He also ate the feast served. By Exodus chapter three this man was the messenger of Jehovah. This messenger appeared again in Judges and in Zechariah. The Father was in the Old Testament; the Son was there; and the Spirit was also there. This is not like modalism, which says that in the Old Testament there was only the Father; there was no Son and no Spirit. When we come to the Gospels, we have seen that while it was the Son that came, He came with the Father and by the Spirit. The Son said that He was never alone because the Father was with Him and He was in the Father and the Father was in Him.

This is not all. The Son was conceived of the Holy Spirit and was born of the Spirit. The Spirit was in Him as His essence. At the age of thirty the Spirit furthermore came upon Him to be His power. He lived and moved by this Spirit, and He worked and fought also by this Spirit for the fulfillment of the Father's divine economy.

TWO KEY WORDS—ESSENTIAL AND ECONOMICAL

Essence and *economy* are two most important, key words in the study of the Triune God and the person of Christ. The Lord Jesus could be conceived and born as a God-man because He had God in Him as His essence and element. In addition, at the age of thirty the Holy Spirit came upon Him. This does not mean that before thirty He did not have the Holy Spirit in Him. Indeed, the Holy Spirit was already in Him. The coming of the Holy Spirit upon Him as His power is the economical aspect. There is a distinction between essence and economy. The Holy Spirit was upon Him for three and a half years. He worked and cast out demons by the power of this Spirit; this is the economical aspect. From His conception, through His birth, and through His living on earth, the Holy Spirit was in Him as life; this is the essential aspect.

Because in the past nearly no one knew the distinction between the essential and the economical aspects of the matter, a great heretic came out by the name of Cerinthus. He taught that Jesus was not God and that He was only a man born of Joseph and Mary. It was only at the age of thirty that Christ (i.e., the Spirit) came upon Him as a dove. He worked and cast out demons by this Christ for three and a half years, until He died on the cross, when the Christ left Him. This was why Jesus prayed on the cross, "My God, My God, why have You forsaken Me." The heretical teaching of Cerinthus was a conjecture based upon the two facts of the Holy Spirit coming upon the Lord Jesus at His baptism and the forsaking of God at His crucifixion on the cross. He made a wrong deduction in considering God to be with the Lord Jesus for a period of time and then leaving Him after three and a half years. Cerinthus did not have the revelation. He did not realize that the Holy Spirit's coming upon the Lord Jesus at His baptism and the forsaking of God at His death on the cross were not essential matters but economical matters.

ESSENTIAL TRINITY AND ECONOMICAL TRINITY

Over fifty years ago, Brother Watchman Nee often told us that the Lord Jesus was the Son, but in eternity past He was the Father, and after resurrection He was the Spirit. *Hymns,* #490 was written by him. Verse 5 says:

> Thou, Lord, the Father once wast called,
> But now the Holy Spirit art;

The Spirit is Thine other form,
Thyself to dwell within our heart.

The above verse is written from the economical point of view. A form is a mode. If you do not know that in God's divine economy there is the essential Trinity and there is the economical Trinity, and if you do not know the difference and the distinction between them, you will think that Brother Nee was teaching the heresy of modalism. Essentially speaking, the Triune God is one. But economically speaking, there is the distinction of three. I will not say that there are three modes, for I do not want to be mistaken for a modalist. This is why I use the expression, "distinction of three." In the Lord Jesus' conception, birth, human living, death on the cross, and resurrection, the Triune God was in Him passing through all these processes together with Him. The Father was in Him; the Son was in Him; and the Spirit was in Him. The whole Triune God was in Him. Essentially speaking, the Father and the Spirit never departed from Him. But in the aspect of God's economy, after the Lord Jesus' baptism, the Holy Spirit was upon Him as His power for three and a half years. Then at the time when He was put on the cross, God forsook Him. This is not according to His essence but is according to His economy. Over twenty years ago, I wrote a book in English entitled *The Economy of God*. In this book there is a passage that reads, "Thus, the three Persons of the Trinity become the three successive steps in the process of God's economy" (p. 10). Here I said "three successive steps in the process of God's economy." In the book *The God-Men*, my opposers changed the word "economy" to "existence," making it read that there are three successive steps in God's existence. This is far off from what I wrote. What I said was that the Triune God has three successive steps in His economy. But the opposers changed my words to read that the Triune God has three successive steps in His existence. This is a great misrepresentation! In God's existence there are not three successive steps because the Father, the Son, and the Spirit are coexistent from eternity. Although there are three, yet

They are one God. This is the essential Trinity. But in God's economy, the Triune God has three successive steps. First, the Father planned. Next, the Son came to accomplish what the Father has planned. Last, the Spirit executes what the Father has planned and what the Son has accomplished. This is the economical Trinity. The Triune God, the Father, the Son, and the Spirit, have a distinction in Their existence and economy. Anyone who fails to realize this distinction will drift into heresy. I hope that you can clearly understand this difference so that you will not be deceived by the seemingly right but actually wrong teachings.

TURNING FROM THE VISIBLE PRESENCE
TO THE INVISIBLE PRESENCE

We now come to the Christ in the Acts. Item number one of the outline says that this pneumatic Christ who is in resurrection breathed Himself as breath into the believers. After this He was with them for forty days in a physical form. At times He appeared and at times He disappeared, training them to be accustomed to His invisible presence. When the Lord was with the disciples for three and a half years, His presence was visible. Although the disciples treasured this very much, there was no way for the Lord Jesus to get into them. The Lord Jesus needed to pass through death and resurrection to become the Spirit so He could enter into them. This is why in John 14:20 the Lord says, "In that day you shall know that I am in My Father, and you in Me, and I in you." In His flesh, the Lord Jesus could only be among the disciples, being with them physically; He could not be in them to be with them invisibly. But after His death and resurrection, He became the Spirit and, as breath, He could be breathed into them to be with them eternally. By John 20:22, after He breathed Himself as breath into the disciples, He was in them, and He was with them in an invisible way. But the disciples were neither appreciative nor were they accustomed to this. For this reason, the Lord Jesus stayed with them for forty days to train them to get used to this invisible presence.

The Lord Jesus was visibly present among the disciples for three and a half years. One day He suddenly disappeared. Then, on the evening of resurrection, He appeared again. The disciples were able once more to see Him and to talk with Him. But then, all of a sudden, the Lord hid Himself from them again. Eventually, they felt that they were bored and were not accomplishing anything by staying there. Peter said, "I am going fishing." They said, "We also are coming with you." And they all went fishing. The strange thing was that the Lord Jesus had chased away all the fish. That night they caught nothing. At daybreak the Lord suddenly appeared on the shore and asked them, "Do you have anything to eat?" They answered feebly, "No." Then the Lord told them to spread the net on the right side of the boat. They did, and the net was filled. They woke up to realize that it was the Lord Jesus. When they got onto the shore, they saw a fire of coals there with fish and bread. The Lord called them to come and dine, and He gave them bread and fish. After they ate, the Lord talked with them. But then, in an instant, the Lord Jesus disappeared again. Nobody knew where He went. All these instances were the Lord Jesus' training of His disciples to be accustomed to His invisible presence.

This is not all. Acts 1 says that after His resurrection the Lord appeared to His disciples for forty days, speaking to them concerning the kingdom of God. Formerly all the disciples had a wrong understanding concerning the kingdom. They thought that the kingdom was just a matter of rule and kingship. Hence, when they were together, they asked the Lord if it was the time for Him to restore the kingdom to Israel. During that time the Lord told them that whether this was the time or not was not a question to be answered by Him, for such a matter belongs to the Father's economy. The kingdom that He talked about was not the kingdom according to their concept. What He meant was that the life of God would increase in them until it became a sphere, the reality and sphere of the living of the divine life, which is the church. Romans 14:17

says that the kingdom of God, which today is the church, is not eating and drinking but is righteousness, peace, and joy in the Holy Spirit. Only this is the kingdom of God. They should wait to be baptized by the Holy Spirit, and then they would receive power from above and would be His witnesses both in Jerusalem, and in all Judea and Samaria, and even unto the uttermost parts of the earth. This is not a matter of essence, but a matter of economy.

Item number two of the outline says that after charging the disciples to wait for the Spirit promised by the Father to fall on them so that they could be His witnesses unto the uttermost parts of the earth, the Lord Jesus visibly departed from them according to God's economy and was taken up into heaven. After He was with them for forty days, at times appearing and at times disappearing to train them to be accustomed to His invisible presence, and after He taught them to understand the kingdom of God, He left them and ascended officially and formally to heaven before their eyes. Had not the Lord Jesus breathed Himself into them? Why then did He physically leave them again to be taken up into heaven? We must realize that the ascension here is economical rather than essential.

PERSEVERING IN PRAYER IN THE ESSENTIAL SPIRIT TO BRING IN THE GREAT ACT OF GOD'S ECONOMY

Item number three says that as far as God's essence is concerned, He was still with the disciples by being in them. Hence, they were able to withstand the threat of the Jews and remain in Jerusalem to wait for the promised Spirit of power from God, and the one hundred and twenty people were able to pray in one accord for ten days, cooperating with God's administration in heaven to bring in the great act of God at Pentecost. Here were one hundred and twenty Galileans who were not afraid of the threat of the Jews in Jerusalem and were gathered together to persevere in prayer with one accord. Formerly they could not comprehend the Lord's word concerning His death and were arguing among themselves as to who were the greatest ones among them and who was to sit at His left and at His right. But now they were sober. They were no longer arguing. All one hundred and twenty of them were in one accord, praying earnestly for ten days. This is not a small thing. It would be hard enough for twelve persons to pray together, much less one hundred and twenty. And they were praying for ten days! This was not all. Peter stood up to expound the Bible and did it accurately. This proves that he had the Holy Spirit as his essence within. The ten days of prayer brought in a great act of God at Pentecost. This was a great move in God's economy. It was something God desired to execute in heaven, but it needed man's prayer on earth. By the Holy Spirit in them essentially, one hundred and twenty people were able to pray earnestly in one accord for ten days. This brought in the great move of God in His economy.

Item number four says that at Pentecost, this exalted God-man, who has ascended to the throne to be made Lord and Christ and Head of all things, poured Himself out as the Spirit of power. On the day of Pentecost, it was not a breathing, but an outpouring. These disciples had already received the Spirit of life, but they were still waiting for the Spirit of power. The Spirit of life is for existence; it is essential. The Spirit of power is for work; it is economical.

Following this, item number four continues by saying that the Spirit of power was poured out on those disciples who had already received Him as the Spirit of life and who were waiting for the Spirit of power. In this way the ascended Head baptized His Body into Himself as the all-inclusive Spirit. First, at Pentecost the Jewish part of the believers was baptized into the Spirit. Then at the house of Cornelius, the Gentile part of the believers was also baptized into the Spirit. In this way, the whole Body of Christ was baptized into this all-inclusive Spirit.

BEING FILLED INWARDLY BY THE SPIRIT OF LIFE AND OUTWARDLY BY THE SPIRIT OF POWER

Item number five says that from now on, those who believe in Him are filled outwardly with His Spirit of power. In Acts when it talks about the filling of the Spirit, it mainly uses two Greek verbs. One is *pletho*, which means an outward filling. The other is *pleroo*, which means an inward filling. We can use the baptistry as an illustration. On the one hand, the water fills the pool inwardly. On the other hand, when you are immersed in the pool, the water does not fill you inwardly, but you are filled by the water outwardly. Both words are used in Acts 2:1-4. Verse 2 says, "Like a rushing violent wind, and it filled [*pleroo*] the whole house where they were sitting." Then verse 4 says, "And they were all filled [*pletho*] with the Holy Spirit." Concerning the house, the wind filled the house inwardly. But concerning the people in the house, the Holy Spirit filled them outwardly. Those who believe in the Lord Jesus are filled outwardly by His Spirit of power and are filled inwardly by His Spirit of life as described in Acts 13:52 where the disciples were said to be filled with joy and the Holy Spirit. Eventually, they were made full of His Spirit. The word "full of" is a third Greek word *pleres*. This is not a verb but an adjective. Examples of usage of this word appear in Acts 6:3, "full of the Spirit and of wisdom," in verse 5, "full of faith and of the Holy Spirit," in 7:55, "full of the Holy Spirit," and in 11:24, "full of the Holy Spirit and of faith." To be "full of" the Spirit is a condition of the believers after having been filled inwardly by the Holy Spirit. Both being "filled" inwardly and "full of" are for life and are essential, while being "filled" outwardly is for work and is economical.

The Lord Jesus was born of the Holy Spirit's conception, having the Holy Spirit as His essence for His existence. At the age of thirty, the Holy Spirit fell upon Him to be His Spirit of power for work. In the same principle, with the disciples on the evening of resurrection, the Lord came to breathe into them for them to receive the Spirit as their life within; this is essential and is for existence. After fifty days, at Pentecost the Holy Spirit was poured out upon them to be the Spirit of power; this is economical and is for work. The Lord Jesus Himself had this twofold experience; the disciples also had this twofold experience; we the believers also have this twofold experience. For a new believer, as soon as he says, "Lord Jesus, I receive You as my Savior," he has the essential Spirit in him as life. By this he can live a spiritual life. At the same time, he can receive the economical Spirit as his outward power to equip him for the Lord's work and testimony.

First Corinthians 12:13 says, "For also in one Spirit we were all baptized into one body, whether Jews or Greeks, whether slaves or free"; this is economical. "And were all given to drink one Spirit"; this drinking is essential and is for our living. The outward baptism of the Spirit is economical and is for work; the drinking in of the Spirit is essential and is for living.

Many times we have this twofold experience. For example, in my daily life, I may be full of meekness, full of the Holy Spirit, full of joy, life, and wisdom. All these came about by the essential Spirit. But now when I have to speak for the Lord, I have to pray, "Lord, I need two aspects. I need the essential Spirit to fill me and to saturate me within, and I need the economical Spirit to fill me without and to clothe me with the heavenly power." By then, I not only have the Spirit of life within; I also have the Spirit of power without. The outward clothing of power is the Spirit of power. It is like the uniform of the policeman, which gives him the authority to carry out his duty.

RECEIVING THROUGH CALLING ON THE NAME OF THE LORD

He who calls on the name of the Lord shall be saved. To believe in the heart and to confess with the mouth by calling is the way to be saved. To be saved does not mean merely to be forgiven of sins; nor does it mean merely to be delivered from perdition. The most important part of salvation is to receive the living Lord, to receive Him as the essential Spirit within as the life for our living and to receive Him as the economical Spirit without as the power for working and fighting for His kingdom. The Spirit of the Lord is like the air. How available and bountiful He is! We can never exhaust His supply. All we need to do is open our mouth to call on His name. This is just like breathing. The Spirit of the Lord will then fill us within. The more we open our mouth to call on the Lord's name, the more we breathe. The more we breathe in this deep way, the more we will be filled inwardly by the Spirit of the Lord. The more we call on the name of the Lord, the more strength we will have. The more we call on His name, the richer will be our life within and the stronger will be our power without. Through calling on the name of the Lord, we will receive the essential and the economical Spirit and will receive it even more abundantly.

FOR THE SPREAD OF HIS KINGDOM AND
FOR THE BUILDING UP OF HIS CHURCH

The last part of item number five says that when the believers are filled inwardly with the Spirit of life and are filled outwardly with the Spirit of power, they become a group of people mingled as one with this all-inclusive Spirit. He is in them as the Spirit of life to be lived out of them to express Himself. He is also outside of them as the Spirit of power to be preached and propagated by them as His continuation and spread on the earth.

Item number six says that those who are filled and saturated with His all-inclusive Spirit within and who are filled and equipped without are led by Him to spread His kingdom on earth that His church may be established. This is indeed glorious! Now at this point, in the Acts we have the church as well as the kingdom. This is the Christ revealed in the book of Acts.

On the one hand, the Lord Jesus acts as Lord and Christ in heaven. On the other hand, He is in us as life and upon us as power that we may live Him. In this way we become His continuation and spread and are made His Body to spread His kingdom and to build up His church.

CHAPTER THREE

CHRIST IN THE EPISTLES

Scripture Reading: Rom. 8:2, 6, 9-11; 1 Cor. 12:13; 3:16; 6:17; 2 Cor. 1:21-22; 3:17-18; 13:14; Gal. 3:14; 1:16; 2:20; 4:19; Eph. 3:8, 17-19; Phil. 1:19-21a; 1 John 2:27; Heb. 7:25; 8:6

OUTLINE

I. Christ, the last Adam, passed through death and resurrection to become the life-giving Spirit—1 Cor. 15:45.

II. Christ, the life-giving Spirit, as the Spirit of life, the Spirit of God, and the Spirit of Christ, who is Christ Himself, first enters into the believers' spirits to make their spirit life. He then spreads from their spirit to their mind, making their minds life also, and finally gives life to their mortal body, so that their whole being—spirit, soul, and body—is saturated by Him as the Spirit of life, and is sanctified and conformed to the image of Him as the firstborn Son of God, to become the many sons of God, being His living members to build up His Body to be His corporate expression—Rom. 8:2, 6, 9-11; 15:16; 8:29; 12:5.

III. After His ascension, He baptized all His believers, whether Jews or Gentiles, in Him as the all-inclusive Spirit into one Body, and made them to drink of one Spirit. In this way they become the temple for Him to dwell in them as the Spirit and are joined to Him as the Spirit to become one spirit, that He may become wisdom to them from God: power, righteousness, sanctification, redemption, and everything—1 Cor. 12:13; 3:16; 6:17; 1:24, 30.

IV. With this all-inclusive Spirit He anoints His believers, sealing them and giving them this Spirit within them as the pledge of their enjoyment of God as their inheritance. This Spirit also becomes the ink (the essence and element) with which is written into them the all-inclusive Christ. As the all-inclusive Lord in resurrection, who is the all-inclusive Spirit, He releases us from the bondage of law and ordinances, that we, with an unveiled face, may behold His glory, may be transformed into His image, from glory to glory, even as from the Lord Spirit. In this way we can enjoy the riches of the Triune God—the grace of Christ, the love of God, and the fellowship of the Holy Spirit—2 Cor. 1:21, 22; 3:3, 17, 18; 13:14.

V. He as the pneumatic Christ, being the blessing of the gospel promised by God, has been revealed in the believers, lives in them, and is being formed in them, that they may live to God by Him as the Spirit—Gal. 3:14; 1:16; 2:20; 4:19; 2:19; 5:25.

VI. He as the pneumatic Christ who has ascended to the heavens and has been exalted by God as the Lord, being the Head of the church, will make His home in the hearts of the believers with His unsearchable riches, that they may be strong to apprehend with all the saints His breadth, length, height, and depth, that they may be filled unto all the fullness of God—the full expression of God, the built up church, as the Body of Christ who fills all in all. This becomes the holy temple of God, the dwelling place of God in our spirit, the universal new man accomplishing God's eternal purpose, the counterpart of Christ satisfying Christ's desire, and the spiritual warrior withstanding God's enemy—Eph. 1:20-23; 3:8, 16-19; 2:21-22; 4:24; 5:31-32; 6:11-13.

VII. He as the pneumatic Christ is also the Spirit of Jesus Christ who was incarnated, put on humanity, passed through human living, died, and resurrected. As such, He has the bountiful supply to enable those who believe in Him and who live in Him to suffer with Him under all kinds of circumstances by His resurrection power and in conformity to His death that they may live Him and magnify Him and be able to do all things in Him through His empowering, gaining Him as the righteousness of God manifested in them—Phil. 1:19-21a; 3:10; 4:13; 3:8-9.

VIII. He as the compound Spirit of such a processed, all-inclusive, life-dispensing Triune God, being typified by the holy ointment in Exodus 30:23-25, abides in us as the anointing of the Triune God, for the purpose that we would abide in the Son and live in the fellowship of the Father, receiving the anointing of this all-inclusive, compound Spirit to enjoy the eternal life, overcoming sin, the world, and Satan, to live out God's inward love and outward righteousness—1 John 2:20, 23-28, 6; 1:5; 3:9; 5:4, 18; 4:7; 5:1; 2:29, 6, 24, 28.

IX. At the same time, He as the ascended Christ is the High Priest in the heavenly tabernacle, interceding for the believers that they would be saved to the uttermost, and being Mediator of the new covenant, executing the testament of the new covenant, supplying the believers with the heavenly life, that they may live a heavenly life on earth and may cooperate with Him as the heavenly Christ to carry out His heavenly ministry on earth—Heb. 4:14-16; 7:25-26; 8:1-2; 7:22; 8:6; 9:15-17.

There are twenty-seven books in the New Testament. In addition to the four Gospels, the Acts, and Revelation, there are twenty-one Epistles. What do these twenty-one Epistles speak about? Bible readers may have read them many times without apprehending the crucial points. However, we must not forget that the subject of the New Testament is Christ. He is a mysterious God-man. These Epistles speak of this God-man in seemingly simple words. The words in these Epistles seem simple, but in their simplicity are hidden deep truths.

CHRIST MAKING HOME IN THE BELIEVERS' HEARTS

As an example of the above, let us consider Ephesians 3:8. Here Paul says that he will preach to us the unsearchable riches of Christ. Literally, this word seems to be very simple. But it is not that easy to understand what are the unsearchable riches of Christ. This phrase means that the riches of Christ are immeasurable. Because it is too mysterious and too inexhaustible to be described in human words, Paul could only use the four dimensions— breadth, length, height, and depth—to describe what Christ is. Christ is the breadth; He is the length, the height, and the depth. The breadth, length, height, and depth of the universe are all unlimited. These are the dimensions of Christ.

In verse 17 Paul said, "That Christ may make His home in your hearts." When Christ makes His home in our hearts and fills and saturates our whole being, we will be strong to apprehend with all the saints what is the breadth and length and height and depth of Christ. The word "make home" here is a compound word in Greek. It is the verbal form of the noun *oikos*, which means house, with the prefix *kata* added to it. *Kata* has the sense of establishing in a firm way. The word is therefore aptly translated as "make home." It is not just an abiding but a making home. I am often invited to different places to conduct conferences. Everywhere I go, the brothers and sisters warmly welcome me. They invite me to stay in their homes and ask me to make myself at home in their homes. I try my best to settle down according to their good wishes. But never have I been able to do so. I can never feel at home in those places. Only when I go back to my own home and put down my luggage can I feel truly at home. Not only do we have to let Christ abide in our hearts, but we also have to let Him make His home deeply in our hearts.

How does Christ make His home in our hearts? For this Paul prayed to the Father. He said that he bowed his knees unto the Father, that He would, according to the riches of His glory and through His Spirit, have Christ make home in our hearts. The meaning of this prayer is very deep. First, it mentions the Father. Second, it mentions the Spirit. Third, it mentions Christ. Lastly, it mentions our heart. We do not have time to go into them in detail·one by one. We can only mention in brief the matter of Christ making home in our hearts.

Our heart is composed of four parts: the mind, the emotion, the will, and the conscience. For Christ to make home in our heart is for Him to make home in these four parts. A home has many rooms, such as the living room and the bedroom. Our heart is the home of Christ. This home has a mind-room, an emotion-room, a will-room, and a conscience-room. We have received Christ into our heart. But is He in our mind, emotion, will, and conscience? Actually, we have often allowed Him to stay only in the living room, not giving Him the liberty to go into the other rooms. The brothers like to exercise their minds. They often remain in their minds. Also they are usually strong in their will. If they say yes, they mean yes. Whether they are right or wrong, they would insist to the end. The sisters are more apt to exercise their emotions. They are often swayed by their joy, their anger, their sorrow, and their elation. All this means that Christ has no place and is not making home in our mind, emotion, and will. We really should have given to Him every room of our heart. Only then will He be able to make home in our heart. All the other tenants in the rooms of our heart have to be chased away. First Corinthians 3:16 says that we are the temple of

God. But this temple is occupied by many illegal tenants. We need the Lord Jesus to chase them away with a whip that this temple may be cleansed; just as He cleansed the temple twice while He was on earth (John 2:14-15; Matt. 21:12), chasing away all the oxen, sheep, doves, buyers and sellers, and money changers. Only then can Christ make His home in our hearts.

Some dissenting ones have said, since we are so small, how can such a great Christ be contained in us? Has not the Bible said that Christ has ascended on high and is seated at the right hand of God with glory as His crown? How then can we say that He lives in our heart? These words seem logical at first hearing. But they are void of the central revelation of the Bible. Romans 8:34 says that Christ has been raised from among the dead and is now at the right hand of God, interceding for us. However, verse 10 of the same chapter says that Christ is also in us. Paul told us that, on the one hand, Christ is in heaven and that, on the other hand, He is in us. This is just like the electricity which is in this meeting hall and is at the same time in the power station. Christ is in us; at the same time, He is in heaven. We should not try to understand Christ with our limited mentality. He is too profound and too unlimited. We can only receive this revelation according to the pure word of the Bible.

CALLING ON THE LORD'S NAME
TO EXPERIENCE CHRIST

Although Christ is so mysterious and unlimited, He is very real and dear. By calling on His name, we can experience Him and be saved by Him in everything in our daily life. The more we call on His name, the more refreshed we feel. This is why we like to call on His name, just as the hymn writer who wrote that we say the sacred name of Jesus a thousand times a day. But again, some dissenting ones condemn this kind of calling. They accuse us of being the callers, saying that this is wrong and is not proper worship. They think that worship is to go to a chapel or cathedral, first to recite some creeds, then to listen to some choirs singing, and then to listen to a sermon by a pastor. Everything should be done according to a program. At the end, the pastor would stretch out his hand to give a benediction, and with the congregation responding with an "amen," the meeting would end, and everybody would go home. Actually, they all come to this kind of meeting empty and leave empty. They receive nothing, and there is no change in their living. This is religion. This is not Christ. We do not need religion. What we need is Christ. The simple way to get Christ is just by calling on His name.

Romans 10:13 says, "Whoever calls upon the name of the Lord shall be saved." This is not just salvation from perdition, but salvation from our temper and disposition as well. To call on the name of the Lord is not a small thing. Many Christians have discovered from their experience that when they are tempted and bothered in their environment and become oppressed and depressed, all they need to do is call on the name of the Lord. Then they will be brought into true fellowship with the Lord and will be able to enjoy the overcoming life of Christ. In this way they will be delivered from their self, sins, the world, the Devil, and all other entanglements, and they will experience Christ as their inward satisfaction and joy.

THE SUBJECT OF THE EPISTLES— THE LAST ADAM BECOMING THE LIFE-GIVING SPIRIT

We have seen the Christ in the Gospels. We have also seen the Christ in Acts. Now we come to the Christ in the Epistles. Item number one of the outline says that Christ, the last Adam, passed through death and resurrection to become the life-giving Spirit. This is the most important point of the Epistles. The last Adam, which is the Lord Jesus, has passed through death and resurrection to become the life-giving Spirit. This life-giving Spirit is the Holy Spirit, because in the whole universe only the Holy Spirit can give life, and this life-giving Spirit is just Christ. Hence, the Christ in the Epistles is the last Adam becoming the life-giving Spirit. This is the subject of the

Epistles. The Christ spoken of in the twenty-one Epistles is the life-giving Spirit. I have selected eight out of these twenty-one Epistles. They are Romans, 1 and 2 Corinthians, Galatians, Ephesians, Philippians, 1 John, and Hebrews. Let us now take a look at the Christ spoken of in these eight Epistles.

The Christ in Romans—the Spirit of Life

Item number two says that Christ, the life-giving Spirit, is the Spirit of life. In Romans 8:2 we have the Spirit of life. Then in verse 9 we see that this Spirit of life is the Spirit of God and the Spirit of Christ, who is also Christ Himself. This pneumatic Christ first enters into the believers' spirit to make their spirit life (Rom. 8:9-10). He then spreads from their spirit to their mind, making their minds life also, and finally gives life to their mortal body, so that their whole being—spirit, soul, and body—is saturated by Him as this Spirit of life to be sanctified and conformed to the image of Him as the firstborn Son of God, to become the many sons of God, being His living members to build up His Body to be His corporate expression.

The book of Romans deals with this Spirit of life, who is the Spirit of God, the Spirit of Christ, even Christ Himself, and the firstborn Son of God. Christ is the Spirit. When He enters into our spirit, He makes our spirit life. Then He spreads from our spirit to the most important part of our soul, which is the mind, that our mind would also have life. He then spreads further outward to dispense His life to our mortal body, that our body would also have life. As a result, we are sanctified and are conformed to His image. In this way we become the many sons of God and are made His members to be built up to be the Body of Christ which is His corporate expression. This is the Christ in the book of Romans.

The Christ in 1 Corinthians—the Body Christ

Item number three says that after Christ's ascension, He baptized all His believers, whether Jews or Gentiles, in Him as the all-inclusive Spirit into one Body. Once at Pentecost and once at the house of Cornelius, God baptized both the Jewish and the Gentile believers into one Body.

We were baptized into the Body of Christ even before we were born. This is also very difficult to understand, but we accept this for the Bible tells us so. This is similar to Revelation 13:8 which says that the Lamb was slain from the foundation of the world. Humanly speaking, the Lord was killed on the cross about one thousand nine hundred years ago; but in God's eyes, He has been slain from the foundation of the world. In the same principle, at Pentecost and at the house of Cornelius, the Lord Jesus as the Head of the church baptized all His believers throughout the generations, both the Jews and the Gentiles, into one Body in this Spirit.

They are also made to drink of this one Spirit. Today we do not have to seek for the baptism of the Holy Spirit anymore. We were already baptized long ago. What we need to do now is to drink of this Spirit every day. The baptism is once for all, but the drinking is continuous and daily. Our salvation through baptism is also once for all. But after being baptized, we still need to drink of this Spirit every day.

According to our experience, to call on the name of the Lord is to drink of this Spirit. But there is a difference between calling and praying. In Romans 10:13, Paul did not say that whoever prays to the Lord shall be saved. Rather, he said that whoever calls upon the name of the Lord shall be saved. The word "call upon" in Greek is *epikaleo*. It means to call out aloud. Although God is omnipotent and omnipresent, He acts according to certain laws. A seed will surely not grow if it is placed on a table, but it will surely grow when it is put into the soil. This is a law. In order for man to be saved, he has to act according to God's law, which is to believe in the heart, to confess with the mouth, and to call on the name of the Lord. We have to believe in our heart and call with our mouth. When we believe in our heart and call with our mouth, we will be saved. We should not wait until calamities arise before we call on the Lord. Instead, we should learn to call on the Lord every day in our daily life. This kind of calling on the name of the Lord is the drinking of the Spirit. By drinking this Spirit, by our calling on the name of the Lord, we become the temple for Him as the Spirit to dwell in and are joined to Him as the Spirit to become one spirit, that He may become wisdom to us from God: power, righteousness, sanctification, redemption, and everything. This is the Christ spoken of in the book of 1 Corinthians.

The Christ in 2 Corinthians— the Anointing, Sealing, Pledging, and Writing Spirit

Item number four says that with this all-inclusive Spirit He anoints His believers, sealing them and giving them this Spirit within them as the pledge of the enjoyment of God as their inheritance. Now this Spirit is both anointing and sealing us within, and as a result, we have this Spirit as the pledge. This is a proof to us that God is our portion. The anointing ointment is Christ. The seal is Christ. The pledge is also Christ. Item number four goes on to say that this Spirit also becomes the ink with which the all-inclusive Christ is written into us. The ink here refers to the essence and element of God. We write with ink. What is written are the letters, while the essence of the letters is the ink. The Spirit that dwells in us is writing continuously. The letters written are Christ, but the essence of the letters is the Spirit. The more this Spirit writes, the more ink we will have within. The more ink we have, the clearer the letters will become. The more this Spirit writes within us, the more Spirit we will have within, and the more Christ will be expressed.

As the all-inclusive Lord in resurrection who is the all-inclusive Spirit, He releases us from the bondage of law and ordinances, that we, with unveiled face, beholding His glory, may be transformed into His image, from glory to glory, even as from the Lord Spirit. In this way we can enjoy the riches of the Triune God—the grace of Christ, the love of God, and the fellowship of the Holy Spirit. This is the Christ in 2 Corinthians.

The Christ in Galatians—
the Spirit as the Blessing of the Gospel
Promised by God

Item number five says that He, as the pneumatic Christ, is the blessing of the gospel promised by God. This blessing is not the blessing of going to heaven, nor is it merely the blessing of forgiveness of sins. Rather, it is that the Spirit will enter into us to be revealed in us, to live in us, and to be formed in us. Not only is Christ living in us, He has to be formed in us, with the result that we would live to God by Him as the Spirit. This is the Christ in Galatians.

The Christ in Ephesians—
as the Head of the Church Making Home
in the Believers' Heart

He, as the pneumatic Christ, who has ascended to the heavens and has been exalted by God as the Lord, being the Head of the church, will make His home in the hearts of the believers with His unsearchable riches, that they may be strong to apprehend with all the saints His breadth, length, height, and depth, that they may be filled unto all the fullness of God, which is the full expression of Him. When we are filled with the riches of Christ to become the fullness of God, we are all coordinated together to become the full expression of God, which is the built up church as the Body of Christ who fills all in all. This becomes the holy temple of God, the dwelling place of God in our spirit, the universal new man accomplishing God's eternal purpose, the counterpart of Christ satisfying Christ's desire, and the spiritual warrior withstanding God's enemy. This is the Christ in Ephesians.

The Christ in Philippians—
the Spirit with the Bountiful Supply

Item number seven says that He as the pneumatic Christ is also the Spirit of Jesus Christ who was incarnated, put on humanity, passed through human living, died, and resurrected. As such, He has the bountiful supply. There is a background to the use of the word "supply" in Philippians 1:19. In the choral band of the ancient Greeks, the leader of the band had to supply all the needs of the members, including their food, clothing, dwelling places, and instruments, etc. Whatever the members needed was supplied by the leader of the band. The Greek word here refers to that kind of supply. Such supply is a bountiful supply. This is why some good translations render this word the "bountiful supply."

Paul used this word to describe the bountiful supply of the Spirit of Jesus Christ, which supplies all the needs of those who believe in Him and who live in Him so that they can suffer with Him under all kinds of circumstances by His resurrection power and in conformity to His death, thus living Him and magnifying Him, being enabled to do all things in Him through His empowering, and gaining Him as the righteousness of God manifested in us. This is the Christ in Philippians.

The Christ in 1 John— the Anointing

Item number eight says that He as the compound Spirit of such a processed, all-inclusive, life-dispensing Triune God, is typified by the holy ointment in Exodus 30:23-25. This ointment is not merely the pure olive oil, but it is mingled with four kinds of spices. In this compound Spirit is divinity, humanity, human living, the death on the cross, His resurrection, and His ascension. This is the Spirit of Jesus Christ. Not only is He the Spirit of God, the Holy Spirit, and the Spirit of Jesus; He is even the Spirit of Jesus Christ. He is such a compound Spirit. This is why 1 John calls Him the anointing. Oil is of one element; but the anointing ointment is a mingling of many elements.

First John speaks not only about the ointment; it speaks about the anointing. The operation of Christ within us is the anointing. He abides in us as the anointing of the Triune God for the purpose that we would abide in the Son and live in the fellowship of the Father, receiving the anointing of this all-inclusive, compound Spirit to enjoy the eternal life, overcoming sin, the world, and Satan, to live out God's inward love and outward righteousness.

First John repeatedly emphasizes that those who are born of God love others. Those who are born of God love the brothers, and those who are born of God do not practice unrighteousness. Rather, those who are born of God live out righteousness. Love is inward, while righteousness is outward. How can we live such a life? How can we have this inward love and outward righteousness? It is by the anointing within us. This is the Christ in 1 John.

The Christ in Hebrews— the Heavenly High Priest and the Mediator of the New Covenant

The foregoing eight items all speak about Christ being in us. But today Christ is not only in us; He is also in the heavens on the throne.

Item number nine says that, in another aspect, He as the ascended Christ is the High Priest in the heavenly tabernacle, interceding for the believers that they would be saved to the uttermost. Not only so, He is also the Mediator of the new covenant, executing the testament of the new covenant. The whole New Testament is not only a book of covenant; it is also a book of bequests, a will for inheritance. Every item in the New Testament is an inheritance from God to us. Christ comes to execute the bequests of this new covenant, supplying the believers with the heavenly life, that they may live a heavenly life on earth and may cooperate with Him as the heavenly Christ to carry out His heavenly ministry on earth. This is the Christ in the book of Hebrews.

THE ESSENTIAL CHRIST AND THE ECONOMICAL CHRIST

From Romans to 1 John, we have the essential Christ. Eventually in the book of Hebrews we have the economical Christ. Essentially speaking, Christ is in us as our life and everything. As far as the divine economy is concerned, Christ is in heaven executing the bequests of the new covenant. At Pentecost when Peter stood up, it was by the economical Christ that he was filled with the power of the Holy Spirit. But it was by the essential Christ that the one hundred and twenty disciples were able to persevere in prayer with one accord for ten days, with no opinion among them, and no fear of the threat of the Jews. In prayer meetings we need the essential Christ. But when we preach the gospel, we need the economical Christ.

We have seen that this Triune God was incarnated, put on humanity, passed through human living, died, resurrected, ascended on high, and now has become the life-giving Spirit making home in our heart. This Christ who dwells in us is, at the same time, sitting on the throne in heaven. He dwells in us as our essence, and He sits in the heavens to execute God's divine New Testament economy. Today He desires that we cooperate with Him to live Him, express Him, preach Him, and propagate Him that we may accomplish God's eternal purpose. This is the Christ in the Epistles.

CHAPTER FOUR

CHRIST IN REVELATION

Scripture Reading: Rev. 1:4-5; 4:5; 5:6; 1:20; 21:10-23; 22:1-2

OUTLINE

I. The pneumatic Christ in the Epistles is the redeeming Lamb in Revelation, who also has become the Executor of God's New Testament economy—Rev. 5:7-10.

II. The all-inclusive, compound Spirit in the Epistles has become the seven Spirits before God's throne in Revelation. The seven Spirits are the center of the divine Trinity in Revelation, proceeding out from the eternal One and of the redeeming One—Rev. 1:4-5.

III. The seven Spirits are the seven lamps of fire before God's throne for the execution of God's economy in the universe and also the seven eyes of the slain Lamb searching and transfusing the churches— Rev. 4:5; 5:6.

IV. The redeeming Lamb as the High Priest in the holy place with the seven eyes which are the Spirits of the seven lamps of fire of God walks among the churches which are the seven golden lampstands to search and to transfuse all the churches that they would become His testimony, the testimony of Jesus—Rev. 1:12, 13, 20.

V. This One, who is the all-inclusive Head who walks in the midst of the churches to search and to transfuse them, is the Spirit who speaks to the churches, purifying the churches and calling forth the overcomers to enjoy Him that they would overcome the deformed churches to bring in His kingdom—Rev. 2:1, 7, 17, 18, 26-28; 3:7, 12-13, 14, 20-22.

VI. As the Lamb who is God's High Priest, He is also God's particular Messenger to care for Israel, the chosen people of God, and the redeemed saints throughout the generations to execute the prayer of the saints concerning God's economy, to take over the earth in the future, and to descend in glory to claim the whole earth for His kingdom—Rev. 7:2-17; 8:3-5; 10:1-5; 18:1; 11:15.

VII. As the seven eyes of the Executor of God's New Testament economy, He is the seven lamps supported by the seven golden lampstands which are the seven churches to shine forth as the testimony of Jesus. The seven Spirits which are the seven lamps in this age will become the lamp which is the Lamb in the new heaven and new earth from which will shine forth the glory of God—Rev. 21:23.

VIII. The seven Spirits are the lamps of fire in this age executing God's New Testament economy. In the new heaven and new earth, they will become the river to water the holy city of God, the New Jerusalem—Rev. 22:1, 2.

IX. The result of the searching and transfusing of the seven Spirits, which are the seven eyes of the Lamb, is the seven golden lampstands in this age and the holy city, the New Jerusalem, in the new heaven and the new earth. Between these two are the Lamb's wife and the Lamb's army, bringing in the Lamb's kingdom—Rev. 19:7, 8, 14, 19; 17:14; 20:4, 6.

X. In eternity, the redeeming Lamb becomes the Lamb-God out from whom flows the river of water of life, which is the all-inclusive Spirit as the life irrigation. On either side of the river grows the tree of life, which is the all-inclusive Christ as the life supply. In eternity this divine Trinity becomes the life and essence of the redeemed ones that they would be mingled with Him to be His full, complete, and perfect (signified by twelve times twelve) corporate expression in eternity—Rev. 21:1, 2, 10-23.

THE CHRIST WHO DWELLS IN THE BELIEVERS
AND WHO ALSO SITS IN HEAVEN
BEING FOR THE PRODUCING OF THE CHURCH

The wonderful Christ in the Epistles, who is the last Adam, has passed through death and resurrection to become the all-inclusive, life-giving, compound Spirit to enter into our spirit to be our life. By drinking of this Spirit, we are baptized in this Spirit into His Body. Furthermore, through the anointing and sealing of this Spirit, the essence of God is added to us more and more. In this way, Christ is able to make home in our hearts, and we are being filled with the unsearchable riches of Christ to become all the fullness of God, which is the church. In addition to this, through the bountiful supply of this all-inclusive, indwelling Spirit, we are saved in all circumstances to be able to live in Christ every day and to abide in the fellowship of God enjoying the eternal life, and thus overcoming sin, the world, and Satan to live out the inward love and outward righteousness of God.

Furthermore, on the one hand, this Christ who has passed through death, resurrection, and ascension lives in us. On the other hand, He is the High Priest in the heavenly tabernacle making intercession for us that we would be saved to the uttermost. At the same time, as the Mediator of the new covenant, He is in heaven executing for us the bequests of the New Testament, supplying us with the heavenly life, that we may be able to live a heavenly life here on earth and may cooperate with Him to fulfill His heavenly commission here on earth.

This Christ has taken us on to such an extent that we have Him as the life essence within and the power and authority without to be the corporate man, the church. We are now cooperating with Him on earth to execute God's divine economy. Unfortunately, the present age is dark, and the world is full of corruption. Even the church has degraded from the purpose of God and has fallen into confusion. On almost every street and lane of a big city, one can see many so-called churches, but it is difficult to find the expression of the Body of Christ. According to the pure revelation of the Bible, the Body of Christ is uniquely one in the universe, and when this Body is expressed in a locality it is a local church. For example, the church in Jerusalem was the Body of Christ expressed as the local church in the city of Jerusalem. Although there were over a million people living in Jerusalem, and although Acts 21 tells us that there were myriads of believing Jews in that city, there was, however, only one church, which was the church in Jerusalem. This is the purpose and ordination of God.

This pneumatic Christ who is in us, is also in heaven as the Executor of the New Testament and the High Priest higher than the heavens, executing in heaven the heavenly ministry for the purpose of producing a church according to His heart's desire, manifested on earth locality by locality, dealing with God's enemy, and fulfilling God's divine economy. However, the church has degraded and become deformed. In this dark and confused age, in order to purge the deformed church and to recover it back to its original position, the Christ in the Epistles has to become the Christ in Revelation.

ONE SPIRIT BECOMING THE SEVEN SPIRITS
FOR THE EXECUTION OF GOD'S ECONOMY

The Holy Spirit in Revelation is no longer the one Spirit in the Epistles but the sevenfold, intensified Spirit, because the world today is corrupted, and the church is degraded, full of darkness and confusion; even the eyes of man's heart are blinded and cannot see clearly the will of God. This is similar to a person not being able to see clearly under one lamp, and who needs, instead, the shining of seven lamps. This is why the one Spirit in the Epistles has been intensified to become the seven Spirits in Revelation. This sevenfold, intensified Spirit is the shining of the seven lamps of fire, enabling us to see the church clearly according to God's desire.

Item number one of the outline says that the pneumatic Christ in the Epistles is the redeeming Lamb in Revelation, who has become the Executor of God's New Testament economy. The pneumatic Christ in the Epistles is the life-giving Spirit. In Revelation, He has become the redeeming Lamb of God to execute God's economy.

Item number two of the outline says that the all-inclusive, compound Spirit in the Epistles has become the seven Spirits before God's throne in Revelation, the center of the divine Trinity, proceeding out from the eternal One and of the redeeming One. Based on what do we say this? This is based on the fact that the seven Spirits are the seven lamps of fire before the throne of God. They are also the one river that proceeds from the throne of God, the eternal One. Moreover, the seven Spirits are the seven eyes of the Lamb. The seven eyes of the Lamb are surely of the Lamb. Hence, the seven Spirits which are the seven eyes of the Lamb are surely of the Lamb, who is the redeeming One. Therefore, on the one hand, the seven Spirits are out from the eternal One, and on the other hand, they are of the redeeming One.

THE SEVEN LAMPS BEING FOR GOD'S MOVE AND THE SEVEN EYES BEING FOR SEARCHING AND TRANSFUSING THE CHURCHES

Item number three says that these seven Spirits are the seven lamps of fire before God's throne for the execution of God's economy in the universe. In the midst of the universe, there is the throne of God in the heavens. Before the throne of God, there are seven lamps of fire. These seven lamps are for God's move. This is similar to driving at night; when the car is about to move, the two headlights are turned on. Once the lights of the car are switched on, the driver will be able to move clearly in the light. The seven lamps of fire shining before the throne of God are an indication that God is executing His economy.

Item number three continues to say that these seven lamps of fire are the seven eyes of the slain Lamb. The seven lamps are for God's move in the execution of God's economy. The seven eyes are for searching and transfusing the churches. The seven lamps of fire are sent forth into all the earth for the execution of God's economy in the universe, and the seven eyes are on the face of the Lamb, Christ, who is the High Priest, for the searching of the churches' condition. On the one hand, the seven eyes are there to search out the condition of the churches. On the other hand, they are there to supply the need of the churches. Similarly, when I speak to you, not only is my mouth speaking, but my eyes also are there transfusing. Through my eyes I transfuse what is in me. The seven eyes of Christ are for searching and transfusing the churches, while the seven lamps before the throne are for the executing of God's economy. But then, the seven lamps before the throne are the seven eyes on the face of the Lamb. This is indeed a mystery! In Revelation, on the one hand, Christ is the One executing God's economy, and on the other hand, He is the One that searches and transfuses the churches.

Item number four says that the redeeming Lamb, as the High Priest in the holy place, with the seven eyes which are the Spirits of the seven lamps of fire of God, walks among the churches which are the seven golden lampstands, to search and to transfuse all the churches, that they would become His testimony, the testimony of Jesus. This is shown in Revelation 1. In this chapter, you can see the seven lampstands and one High Priest walking in the their midst. His eyes are as a flame of fire searching the churches and, at the same time, supplying all the churches' needs.

SPEAKING TO THE CHURCHES TO PURIFY THEM AND TO CALL FORTH THE OVERCOMERS

Item number five says that this One who is the all-inclusive Head who walks in the midst of the churches to search and to transfuse them, is the Spirit that speaks to the churches, purifying the churches and calling forth the overcomers to enjoy Him, that they would overcome the deformed churches to bring in His kingdom. This refers to the seven epistles to the seven local churches in Revelation 2—3. Each of these seven epistles opens with the words that these epistles are spoken to the churches by the One who is the Lord Christ, the Head, the One walking in the midst of the churches, and the Christ who holds the seven stars. But at the end of every epistle, it says that these words are spoken by the Spirit to the churches and "he who has an ear, let him hear." This proves that the Spirit and Christ are one. The totality of all the words in the seven epistles is for the purifying of the churches and for the calling forth of the overcomers to enjoy Christ. The Spirit says to the church in Ephesus that to him who overcomes will be given to eat of the tree of life, which is in the paradise of God (Rev. 2:7); to the church in Pergamos, to him who overcomes, will be given of the hidden manna (Rev. 2:17); to the church in Laodicea, to him who overcomes, He says, "I will come in to him and dine with him and he with Me" (Rev. 3:20). To eat of the tree of life, to partake of the hidden manna, and to dine with the Lord are all matters of enjoying Christ. All three kinds of enjoyment are typified in the Old Testament. The first kind is the tree of life recorded in Genesis 2. The second kind is the manna recorded in Exodus 16. The third kind is the produce of the good land as the feast for all to dine, as recorded in Deuteronomy 8. Therefore, in His promise to the overcomers, He has included the three highest enjoyments of the Old Testament. The tree of life, the hidden manna, and the feast in the good land are all types of the rich enjoyment of Christ. Only by these can we overcome today's deformed church and bring in the kingdom of God.

AS THE PARTICULAR MESSENGER OF GOD FULFILLING GOD'S SPECIAL COMMISSION

Item number six says that as the Lamb who is God's High Priest, He is also God's particular Messenger. He is the High Priest, the Executor, and Mediator of the new covenant. As such, He is also the redeeming Lamb. Revelation 7:2, 8:3, 10:1, and 18:1 all mention another Angel. This another Angel is Christ. In Revelation, as in the Old Testament, Christ is the messenger of God (Gen. 22:11-12; Exo. 3:2-6; Judg. 6:11-24; Zech. 1:11, 12; 2:8-11; 3:1-7) to fulfill God's special commission. This special Messenger cared for the Israelites, the chosen people of God, and has shepherded the redeemed saints throughout the generations, executing the prayer of the saints concerning God's economy. In Revelation 8:3, the Messenger offers the prayers of the saints to God. As a result, God hears the prayers and executes His economy on earth. Not only so, He will come to take over the earth and will descend in glory to claim the whole earth for His kingdom. These are the special commissions of this particular Messenger.

THE SEVEN LAMPS
WHO ARE THE SEVEN SPIRITS IN THIS AGE
BECOMING THE LAMP OF THE LAMB
IN THE NEW HEAVEN AND NEW EARTH

Item number seven says that as the seven eyes of the Executor of God's New Testament economy, He is the seven lamps supported by the seven golden lampstands which are the seven churches. Upon every lampstand are seven lamps, and these seven lamps are the seven eyes of the Lamb. Hence, every golden lampstand supports the seven eyes of the Lamb as the seven lamps, shining forth as the testimony of Jesus. These seven lamps who are the seven Spirits in this age will become the lamp which is the Lamb in the new heaven and new earth. The seven lamps supported by the seven lampstands are the seven Spirits today. In the new heaven and new earth, the lamp in the New Jerusalem will be the Lamb. This does not mean that there are two lamps, but rather, that it is one lamp in two different ages. The Spirit today is the Lamb in the future. Today the Spirit is the lamp. In the future the Lamb will be the lamp. When the Lamb becomes the lamp, the world will no longer be dark, and there will be no more night. But today the world is full of darkness; hence, there is the need for the seven Spirits to be the seven lamps. The seven Spirits who are the seven lamps are Christ Himself. In eternity future in the New Jerusalem the Lamb will be the lamp. This is because in the New Jerusalem in the new heaven and new earth, the old heaven and earth will have passed away, and everything will be made new. In eternity future there will be no darkness, neither will there be night anymore. Therefore, the seven lamps which are the seven Spirits will become the lamp of the Lamb to shine forth the glory of God.

THE SEVEN SPIRITS BEING THE SEVEN LAMPS IN THIS AGE AND THE RIVER OF WATER IN THE NEW HEAVEN AND NEW EARTH

Item number eight says that the seven Spirits are the lamps of fire in this age, executing God's New Testament economy. In the new heaven and new earth, they will become the river to water the holy city of God, the New Jerusalem. Today in the church age, the seven Spirits are the seven lamps for the shining, activating, and executing of God's New Testament economy. But in the age of the new heaven and new earth, they will become the river of water for the supplying, irrigating, and refreshing of the holy city, the New Jerusalem.

THE LAMB'S WIFE AND THE LAMB'S ARMY

Item number nine says that the result of the searching and transfusing of the seven Spirits, which are the seven eyes of the Lamb, is the seven golden lampstands in this age and the holy city, the New Jerusalem, in the new heaven and the new earth. In between these two, there is the Lamb's wife for His satisfaction, and there is the Lamb's army to fight with Him to bring in the Lamb's kingdom.

THE TRIUNE GOD AS THE LIFE AND ESSENCE OF HIS REDEEMED ONES, MINGLING WITH THEM TO BE THE CORPORATE EXPRESSION OF HIM IN ETERNITY

Item number ten says that in eternity the redeeming Lamb becomes the Lamb-God. In Revelation 22:1 it says that God and the Lamb sit on one throne. For God and the Lamb both to occupy one throne is a problem that puzzles many who study the Bible. Only by reading it in its context can we understand this kind of expression. It is by

God being in the Lamb that They can sit on one throne, because chapter twenty-one says that God is the light and the Lamb is the lamp. The light is in the lamp; therefore, God is in the Lamb. It is by this that God and the Lamb can be sitting on the same throne. In other words, God and the Lamb are one. This is also to say that the redeeming God is the Lamb-God. From this Lamb-God flows the river of water of life, which is the all-inclusive Spirit as the life infusion. On the two sides of the river grows the tree of life, which is the all-inclusive Christ as the life supply. The river of life is the Spirit, and the tree of life is Christ. This is the divine Trinity becoming the life and essence of the redeemed ones in eternity, enabling them to be mingled with Him as one to be His corporate expression in eternity that is full, perfect, and complete.

Today the church is in a dark and confusing age, and Christ is the all-inclusive, sevenfold, intensified Spirit. Hence, to be a Christian in this age, we should not only analyze the biblical doctrines merely with our mind, but we should exercise our spirit to read the Lord's Word, which is the Bible. If we would turn every word that we read into prayer, the words will be in us as the supplying Spirit and the shining light. By pray-reading the Lord's Word and enjoying the supply of the Spirit this way, we will be filled with the Holy Spirit and full of light. We do not need the dead letters and doctrines, but we need the living Spirit and the light of life. We must touch the living Spirit and enjoy the light of life through pray-reading the Lord's Word. In this way, the one Spirit who indwells us is intensified to become the seven Spirits, and every local church is a golden lampstand as the embodiment of the Triune God.

The golden lampstand has gold as its essence, signifying that the Father is the source and the nature. The shape of the lamp has a form, signifying that the Son is the embodiment and expression of the Father. The seven lamps signify the Spirit as the manifestation and the shining. Therefore, the golden lampstand is the embodiment of the Triune God as the Father, the Son, and the

Spirit. In this age, the golden lampstands are the local churches. A local church must be full of the Spirit to be the bride as the counterpart of the Lamb to satisfy His heart and also to be the Lamb's army following Him and fighting with Him, defeating Antichrist to bring in the Lamb's kingdom. In the end, the New Jerusalem will come down from heaven to be the ultimate expression of the Triune God. The New Jerusalem is composed of the mingling of the Triune God with all His redeemed people. God is the life and the essence within His redeemed ones, and His redeemed ones become a city without, to express God's effulgence, that is, the glory of God.

THE ETERNAL HABITATION OF GOD

The New Jerusalem is the ultimate expression of the church and is built of three kinds of material: gold, precious stones, and pearls. Gold signifies the nature of God the Father. Pearls signify the result of the redemption of God the Son. The precious stones signify the result of the transformation of God the Spirit. Hence, the New Jerusalem bears the nature of God the Father, the result of God the Son's redemption, and the work of transformation of God the Spirit. The New Jerusalem, composed of these three persons, becomes God's eternal habitation, with God in it as its source. As the One sitting on the throne, He is the Lamb-God, the redeeming God, from whom flows the river of water of life, which is the Spirit. On either side of the river is the tree of life, which is the Son. Here we have the Father as the source, the Spirit as the flow, and the Son as the life supply to meet all the needs of the entire city. Hence, everything related to this city is life and light. By then, the New Jerusalem will have become the full expression of the Triune God, expressing Him forever in eternity future. This is the Christ revealed in the book of Revelation. It is also the ultimate revelation of the whole Bible concerning Christ.